The
Power
of
Self-Esteem

Other Books by Wally Amos
Published by
Blue Mountain Arts®

Be Positive! Be Positive!
Insights on How to Live
an Inspiring and Joy-Filled Life

Live an Inspiring Life:
10 Secret Ingredients for Inner Strength

The

Power

of

Self-Esteem

How to Discover and
Fulfill Your Life Dreams

Wally Amos

with Stu Glauberman

Blue Mountain Press®

Boulder, Colorado

Library of Congress Catalog Card Number: 2006007628
ISBN-13: 978-1-59842-170-5
ISBN-10: 1-59842-170-0

Certain trademarks are used under license.
BLUE MOUNTAIN PRESS is registered in U.S. Patent and Trademark Office.

Printed in the United States of America.
First Printing: 2006

 This book is printed on recycled paper.

This book is printed on fine quality, laid embossed, 80 lb. paper. This paper has been specially produced to be acid free (neutral pH) and contains no groundwood or unbleached pulp. It conforms with all the requirements of the American National Standards Institute, Inc., so as to ensure that this book will last and be enjoyed by future generations.

Library of Congress Cataloging-in-Publication Data

Amos, Wally.
     The power of self-esteem : how to discover and fulfill your life dreams / Wally Amos with Stu Glauberman.
        p. cm.
     ISBN 1-59842-170-0 (trade pbk. : alk. paper) 1. Self-esteem. 2. Success—Psychological aspects. I. Glauberman, Stu. II. Title.

     BF697.5.S46A46 2006
     158'.1—dc22

                                                            2006007628

Blue Mountain Arts, Inc.

P.O. Box 4549, Boulder, Colorado 80306

Contents

Introduction

I have been thinking and writing about self-esteem for a long time. It's ironic that my advice is sought on the subject because sixty-plus years ago, I was a high school dropout and I sorely needed a lecture on raising myself up, but nobody gave it to me. I could have used some good advice in the 1960s and the 1970s, too. Happily, with help, I finally figured it out for myself and, with a little help, you can do the same.

This volume echoes what I've written in *Live an Inspiring Life* and other books. Though I've discussed the topic of self-esteem many times before, I'm always filled with enthusiasm and new ideas about it. If you know anything about me, apart from the fact that I love cookies, you probably know that I'm high on high self-esteem.

Some social scientists are now arguing that the "self-esteem thing" has gone too far by promising too much. They cite studies showing that high self-esteem does not necessarily translate into high grades in schoolchildren and that adults with high self-esteem aren't always the most productive workers or the best leaders. It seems the latest pop-psychology position is aimed at putting down the power of self-esteem.

I have to laugh because I've been saying all along that you can't let anyone put you down or tell you what to think. I'm not pushing self-esteem as the cure-all for everything that ails you or as a magic potion for making you the smartest student in the class or the most successful person on the planet. I'm just emphasizing that self-esteem is one of the secret ingredients you need to discover and fulfill your life's dreams. Some of the other ingredients necessary to create and realize your dreams are a positive attitude, commitment, integrity, the gift of giving, imagination, enthusiasm, faith, and that old standby, love.

Trust me, you'll get a lot farther on a gallon of high self-esteem than you will on a tankload of low self-esteem. Coupled with your other good qualities, positive self-esteem will help you flourish and become the best you can be.

The comedian George Carlin once quipped that most people with low self-esteem have earned it. I think that if you recognize your problem, you're on your way to solving it.

The power in you begins with self-esteem. So let's get started!

Up from the Depths

Ask yourself these questions: Who are you allowing to tell you how to live your life? Are you happy with the results? Do you even know who you are? Why are you allowing others to mold your opinions of yourself and make choices for you?

Years ago, I would have failed this personality test hands down. I wasn't happy with who I was; in fact, I didn't *know* who I was or how special I was. I had never thought of taking control of my destiny or making my own choices. I was clueless and dreamless. Like a train without a track, a steamboat without steam, or a rocket without a fuse, I was going nowhere fast. My self-esteem was on empty.

To hold something in esteem means to hold it in favorable regard, to consider it valuable. Self-esteem is to hold yourself in high regard, to think of yourself as a hot property, a uniquely valuable individual, a one-of-a-kind collector's item.

In 1948, I was sent up north to live with my Aunt Della and Uncle Fred in Harlem. I was a twelve-year-old skinny black kid from Tallahassee whose parents were getting a divorce. I wasn't motivated to do anything or be anything. I saw little value in myself. I had arrived in the Big Apple thinking I was the pits. I had already been conditioned and molded to believe that others were better than me. In the multiracial, multiethnic stewpot that was New York City, I found myself critically measuring my Florida-born, country-boy self against the Chinese, Irish, Italian, Jewish, Puerto Rican, and hip, citified black kids in my junior high school — and I found myself sorely lacking. Although I didn't know it, the only things I really lacked were self-confidence and self-esteem. I didn't realize it at the time, but I was stacking the deck against myself and dealing myself a low hand.

Where did I get the notion that I wasn't as good as others? I was raised in Tallahassee's "colored" section, a closed society with little outside input. Strange to say, but it wasn't outsiders that were putting me down. All the ideas I had about the world came from my parents and our own community. Despite the positive teachings I got from the Bible, my view of my own worth was negative. This was largely because I couldn't meet my parents' exacting standards, and they let me know it. When I didn't live up to my mother's expectations, she whipped me. It's hard to get a sense of self-worth from painful lessons like that. Only later in life did I discover the importance of realizing and celebrating self-worth, of defining your own place in the universe, and of understanding that each of us is invested with merit and worth as part of God's plan.

Luckily, my Aunt Della's love for me was unconditional. Even so, what I needed was some love of myself by me and for me. Can you say you love yourself? Loving yourself is essential to loving and being loved by others.

As my friend Dr. Wayne Dyer says, "You cannot be lonely if you like the person you're alone with." Discover for yourself what you have to offer. Allow time to be by yourself and with yourself. Take time to appreciate you.

Once you begin to believe in yourself, others will begin to believe in you. Once you place a high value on yourself, others will value you as well.

Enjoy your uniqueness. Out of all the billions of people since the beginning of time, there has never been, and never will be, another you. Take some time to identify the things that make you unique. Each day you can work on finding new ones. Write them down and continue to affirm them.

As you lift yourself up, you'll find that your attitude toward the world hinges on how you look upon yourself. The world outside becomes a reflection of what you are within. But don't take yourself too seriously.

Learn to laugh at yourself and forgive yourself. Be compassionate with yourself.

My wife, Christine, and I used to go to a lot of self-realization seminars. They taught us various methods for getting in touch with our inner selves. Eventually, it occurred to me that you can't get in touch with your inner self by reading a book or using someone else's rules. Finally, I said to Christine, "I'm not going to any more seminars. I'm going to *live* the stuff of these seminars. I'm going to apply it."

You don't know if a lesson is valuable until you put it to work for yourself.

Today, there are lots of self-esteem and self-help courses and seminars. They begin by telling you to listen to a little voice inside you. I say tune in to your inner voice and let it roar. But take it from me: you can't buy self-esteem right off the shelf. You've got to work for it.

Learning to Dream

Finding work was never really a problem for me. Finding value in myself was the problem. As a kid in Tallahassee, I delivered newspapers and shined shoes. After moving to New York City, I delivered groceries, ice, and more newspapers. I dropped out of high school and joined the Air Force. Upon leaving the Air Force, I attended secretarial school and worked as a stock clerk at Saks Fifth Avenue, ultimately becoming the supply department manager. Due to a profound lack of commitment and the negative notion that divorce ran in my family, I also dropped out of my first marriage and, later, my second marriage. I was careful not to make the mistake of dropping out of the lives of my three young sons.

Eventually, I took control of the wheel and steered myself toward considerable success in the material world. I began to work for the William Morris Agency, first as a mailroom clerk and then as a secretary. This was actually the first time I saw an opportunity for a career. In less than a year, I became a theatrical agent. What do you know? By staying positive and steering a steady course, I sailed through a series of work-related situations and developed self-confidence. In this way, I came upon the ability to define myself and dream for myself.

In 1975, I dreamed myself into the crazy idea of opening the world's first store devoted solely to selling chocolate-chip cookies. I was an inexperienced thirty-nine-year-old novice in the cookie-baking business, but I had my Aunt Della to thank for introducing me to her tried, true, and most delicious recipe. I also had some friends in the entertainment business to thank for backing me.

I opened the first Famous Amos Chocolate Chip Cookie store on Sunset Boulevard and soon I was rolling out — and rolling in — the dough. By 1980, I was making $5 million a year. Suddenly, the no-count boy from Harlem was a success and a Hollywood celebrity. I was "Famous Amos," the bewhiskered brown face that launched a thousand chips. Before long, my battered Panama hat and my trademark Indian embroidered pullover shirt were installed in the Smithsonian Institution's Business Americana exhibit celebrating America's entrepreneurial spirit. I was truly a part of history, but the Wally Amos belief system was still evolving.

Perhaps you are like I was and you're putting too much weight on what you think you lack and not enough on what you have.

To harness the power of self-esteem and make
it work for you, begin by acknowledging that
you have the free will and free choice to
take full responsibility for who you are,
how you see yourself, and what
direction you're going to point
yourself in. There's only one person
who can lift your low self-esteem and raise it up to the
heights of self-love and self-confidence, and that's you.

*Stop being your own worst
enemy and start being your
own best friend.*

Setting a High Value on Self-Worth

How many times a day do you think about your self-worth? Believe it or not, I was in my late forties when I first considered the concept of self-worth. The topic came up in a Unity Church sermon when the minister impressed upon the members of the congregation just how fantastic they were. Growing up, it never dawned on me that I was fantastic. If I ever expressed a positive thought, someone was always there to put me down or challenge me with the question or the dirty look that asks, "Who do you think you are?" I was told so many times that I was a selfish, no-count kid that I began to think I didn't count. That's true for many of us. I once signed an autograph for a woman, "You are special!" and I underlined the "You" to emphasize it. She looked at me with tears in her eyes and said, "No one ever said that to me before." She had a bad case of low self-esteem.

I had never heard of self-esteem before mine fell to its lowest level, and I never knew what an inferiority complex was, even though I had one.

Many people blame their low self-esteem and feelings of inferiority on others, such as parents or peers who told them they were lousy, rotten kids. There is a degree of blame to be shared between the tellers and the person being told.

I've come to understand that you cannot have low self-esteem thrust upon you without your permission. You can't be stepped on again and again unless you agree to lie down and stay there and let people step all over you.

Just when it seems you're out of luck or out of energy, the universe will come through with an opportunity, insight, or inspiration. I believe that if you have a positive attitude, the universe will provide. Throughout my life, when mistakes led me into darkness, a positive experience or a brilliant new idea showed me the way out.

What to Do When You Hit Bottom

Do you remember what it is like to be a kid sliding down a waterslide? Frightened or not, you know instinctively that you're going to hit bottom. And even the smallest child knows that when you reach the bottom, you've got to stand up.

If you lose touch with the power that's in you, it's easy to slide into the abyss of despair. But if you think hard and look closely, you'll find there's always a lifeline to latch on to and pull yourself up.

Sometimes when you start thinking things aren't going your way, you count all the "bad things" that are happening and total them up with the certainty that nothing good will happen. It's like pushing yourself down a hill or kicking yourself when you're already down.

There are times when we can all relate to the title of songwriter and poet Richard Fariña's 1960s novel *Been Down So Long It Looks like Up to Me*. There are many excuses for being down, but if you take a positive attitude, things can only look up from there. How long should you allow yourself to stay down? Don't wait for the ten-count. Don't wait a minute longer than it takes to stand up.

In his hit song, "Limbo Rock," when Chubby Checker asked "How low can you go?" he wasn't challenging people to go from bad to worse. He was encouraging them to bend their backs and emerge triumphantly limber from under the limbo pole. Sometimes it may seem you'll never be able to bend and come out from under the barriers that are getting you down. The only way to overcome obstacles is to continue working your way through them.

No one ever issued an insurance policy to guarantee that life would be easy.

When everything seems to be at its gloomiest, remember that the darkest hour is just before the dawn. Seen another way, the darkest hour is precisely the time for you to shine, because it's in the darkest sky that you get the best view of the stars. After that, you can enjoy the quiet beauty of dawn and the start of a bright, new day.

Instead of asking yourself, "Why is everything so difficult for me?" ask, "Is it possible?" The answer will always be "yes," because all things are possible if you have faith, patience, and the will to accomplish whatever it is that you desire.

Years ago, I learned that life is never really what it seems. It's always more!

You always have the choice: pick yourself up off the floor, get up and go forward, or lie there and play dead. If you choose to move ahead, you are emancipated; from that point on, you are 100 percent responsible for your self-image.

Someone e-mailed me an anonymous poem titled "The Road to Success." In this poem, the author writes that the road to success is not straight. One curve leads to failure, another leads to confusion. Friends and relatives are the speed bumps and flashing, yellow caution lights along the way. Sometimes your job will seem like a flat tire, and to get back on the road and reach your destination, you'll need a spare tire called *determination*, an engine called *perseverance*, and an insurance policy called *faith*. To this, I would add that the bumpy road you travel will feel smoother if you pack a *positive attitude* to bolster your belief in yourself, plus plenty of *enthusiasm* for whatever lies ahead. And don't wait by the roadside for success to come along like a crosstown bus. Go out and find it, flag it down, and jump aboard.

Sometimes all you need to get yourself in high gear is a new idea. Seize it and let it take you for a ride.

The Lessons of Watermelon

By now, the whole world knows I love chocolate-chip cookies. In 1996, I confessed that I also love watermelon. In my book *Watermelon Magic*, I explored the circumstances that led to the ridiculous idea that if you were black, it was somehow laughable and shameful to eat watermelon. I don't remember ever being told this, but I knew it and every other black person seemed to know it, too. We were all imprisoned by a meaningless stereotype that was foisted upon us for no logical reason.

Apparently, the stereotype goes back more than a century, even before photographers went south to capture it. The lithographs of the highly respected Currier & Ives Company carried this image of blacks eating watermelon into white American homes in the 1880s, and the superficially funny "Our Gang" comedies perpetuated it half a century later.

What made blacks eating watermelon an object of scorn when millions of whites were enjoying watermelon at picnics and at home in their parlors? There is no rational explanation except that one group sought to oppress another using ridicule as a tool.

Stereotypes aren't restricted to race and religion. Gender and sexual orientation are also easy targets for fundamentalists who do not embrace the humanity of all human beings. And isn't it amazing that our society praises a man for being forthright and aggressively pursuing his viewpoint, but heaps scorn on and has ugly words for women who express themselves directly and act on their own behalf? Stereotypes rooted in prejudice and based on the color of one's skin, one's beliefs, or unfair traditions — such as women not being allowed to hold positions traditionally held by men — are a plague on any group or community that tolerates them.

False beliefs can become an obstacle to your self-esteem only if you allow them to stand in your way.

Eleanor Roosevelt was right when she said, "No one can make you feel inferior without your permission." That's why I strongly believe in breaking the chains of ignorance and living unbound by stereotypes. I also believe in the inalienable right to eat watermelon, and I don't really care what others may think about it. It's up to me to determine what I like to eat, think, and do. It's up to you to decide what you like to eat, think, and do and to assert your right to revel in those things. One of the best books I've read is *What You Think of Me Is None of My Business* by Terry Cole-Whittaker. The title alone can be life changing.

> *My advice to you is never to let the negative opinions of others place a value on who you are and what you're worth.*

It's okay to like what you like and do what you do. It doesn't matter what other people think you should like and not like, and do and not do. It's okay to love watermelon simply because it is so delicious. Despite what others will say, you can love to eat your comfort foods and wear your comfortable clothes no matter what color your skin is, who your parents are, what your sexual orientation is, or what you do for a living. This is also true about making your own decisions; it's okay to do what you think is best for you.

Who cares what others think of you or what you're doing? You certainly shouldn't. And it's okay to make mistakes even if others choose to scoff. Making mistakes is as natural as slipping on a banana peel or falling out of bed. There is no one on earth who hasn't made a misstep and fallen on his or her face.

One of the most important lessons in life is that you count and what you think counts. It takes everyone and everything and every idea to make the universe whole.

Unfortunately, it takes some people a lifetime before they realize it's okay to speak their minds. Many people spend their whole lives waiting for wisdom and experience and only find their voices to say what they really think when they have already lost their teeth. I agree with Oprah Winfrey who has done more for self-esteem than anyone else on television. She advises that it's more important to say what you believe than it is to hold your tongue to keep the peace or please others.

Learning to express what you think is another step toward building your self-confidence and being all that you can be.

Wally Goes to the White House

I have learned from my own life experience that formal education is not the only valuable form of education. When I was a talent agent at William Morris, I had a secretary with a college degree who couldn't spell as well as I could. It occurred to me then that getting through college doesn't mean you're smart, it only means you got through college. Once I was being interviewed on a radio talk show and a woman called in with a question. She told me she held a PhD and her husband held an MBA, and then she proceeded to ask me, a high school dropout, for advice on starting a business.

Some people look down on others who are not as highly educated as they are, believing them to be of less worth. The outstanding *American Experience* series on PBS presented the remarkable true story of Vivien Thomas, a lab technician at the Johns Hopkins School of Medicine. Without any college training, Thomas invented unique surgical tools and helped pioneer a surgical technique to prevent so-called "blue babies" from dying of a congenital heart defect. A black man, Thomas was praised as a genius and a brilliant teacher by the all-white medical staff at the segregated hospital campus in the 1940s, yet he was not allowed to eat in the same lunchroom or enter the Baltimore hotel where they celebrated the life-saving technique he helped develop.

Think of yourself as an innovator in your own life. You are a human being with as much human potential as your neighbor, your supervisor, or your president.

In 1986, I was invited to participate in the White House Conference on Small Business. When the time came to meet President Ronald Reagan at a White House reception, I was the only participant dressed in a Hawaiian shirt and a Panama hat. I was also probably the only person entirely at ease about being a guest at the White House.

Immediately upon entering the historic residence, a symbol of American might, I realized that its enormous power comes from the office and not the office-holder. The great POTUS (the diplomatic abbreviation for president of the United States) is just a human being like you and me. I had nothing to fear, no reason to feel small, and no reason to be anyone but myself.

The one thing we all have in common is that we are spiritual beings having human experiences. Our humanness is far more important than the color of our skin, religion, gender, or status.

The world would be a better place
if we focused more on
our similarities and less on
our differences.

Biologically there is so little difference between us. Ideologically, we have great differences, but these can be bridged with compassion and understanding. Think about this: our faces are different, but our hearts are all the same. There are no black hearts, white hearts, or yellow hearts, only hearts filled with love to share.

Later, while we were having photographs taken, I took out a dollar bill and asked President Reagan to autograph it to Aloha United Way so it could be auctioned off to raise money for the charitable organization. At that moment, he wasn't the president of the United States; he was just a person looking to fulfill my wish. For me, it was a defining moment that will have meaning for the rest of my life. At the charity auction, the bill brought in $50.

Ask any businessman and he'll tell you that a fifty-to-one return on an investment isn't bad. I was glad I'd had the courage to ask. My friend, Del Smith, says, "If you don't a-s-k you will never g-e-t."

Years ago, I thought of myself in terms of my title. Whenever I had business cards made, I described myself as "President and Founder." Then, after hearing a life-changing talk by Dr. Lance Secretan about his destiny, cause, and calling, it occurred to me that the business of my life is more than just a business. I have a mission in life beyond putting flour in the pantry and dough in the bank, a purpose that is not related to the particular business venture or ventures I happen to be involved in at the time. I have a larger mission. Realizing my higher purpose, I decided that my title should reflect my destiny, my cause, and my calling in life. After much thought, I determined that my destiny is to elevate self-esteem in our society. My cause is to inspire people to feel good about themselves. My calling in life is to inspire people by being a positive example. Therefore, rather than "President" or "Chairman," my title is "Messenger of Inspiration."

No matter what you do for a living, you can contribute to the betterment of our society simply by inspiring someone else.

Take it from me, you reap the reward whenever someone says, "You inspired me." What is your destiny? What is your cause? What is your calling? If you could choose a title for what you want to be in this life, what would it be?

Born to Be Perfect

Some people imagine themselves to be lacking because they don't have the designer clothes, the big house with a picket fence, or the sports car or private jet they were conditioned to want. Wanting material things is the high-octane fuel that keeps the fires of low self-esteem burning. If you fancy that you need fancy things to give yourself value, you will probably never have enough things and never value yourself.

The antidote to this addictive poison is to focus on the God-given things that you had when you were born. Whenever I think of how all of us come into this world as children, I am overwhelmed by the perfection of it all. I was busy being busy when my sons were born and missed being present at their births, though it was also the case that fathers were not permitted in the delivery room in those years. A little over twenty years ago, after the rules had changed and I had become more worldly, more mature, and more certain of myself, I made certain I was present for the birth of my daughter.

When I saw Sarah being born, I had an epiphany. We are absolutely complete from the moment we are born. We enter the universe with everything we need. After that, we just get bigger and better at being who we are. Think about it. From the very start, you were programmed and hard-wired to grow into a child, an adolescent, and then an adult. You were born with all the bodily parts and functions you need to succeed. The same can be said for every healthy child born to every healthy parent in every country of the world, from the first day of Creation until today.

To this day, I get choked up when I think about the miracle of Sarah's birth — and every birth — and the endless possibilities of what we can achieve. Thinking more about your birth can do wonders to elevate your self-esteem and help you create a new and improved you.

All you really have to do with your God-given self is work it, develop it, and improve on what you have.

Realize that you are important to the entire world; what happens to the world begins with you.

Anchors Aweigh

Are you the kind of person who lets rainy days and Mondays get you down? Where I live in Hawaii, the weather is nearly perfect most of the time when the trade winds blow. It's so nice so often that when the trade winds fail and the sky clouds up or it rains for more than a day or two, some people get grouchy. Psychologists call this condition Seasonal Affective Disorder, or SAD for short. They say that prolonged bad weather can lead to depression and dampen your enthusiasm, leaving you feeling blue. I'm no psychologist, but it occurs to me that both the disorder and the cure are in the mind. All you've got to do is choose to think and act positively and find something interesting to do. If the sky is black and the rain won't stop, grab a philosophical umbrella and let the sun figuratively shine in. You can shop if you like to shop, spend time with friends who are fun to be with, or curl up with a good book. Whatever you do, if you do it with a sunny attitude inside, you can beat the weather outside. You'll suffer from JOY instead of SAD. Joy comes from within.

Many people allow themselves to be dominated willy-nilly by the words and actions of others. Unfortunately, these individuals remain imprisoned by OPTs — other people's thoughts — when they could be exerting their willful resolves to free themselves from outside influences.

When we refuse to think and act on our own behalf, we yield to others the ability to create our opinions of ourselves.

Why allow someone else to build or destroy your self-image? Why give someone else the opportunity to drop an anchor over your shoulders and weigh you down? Why volunteer to take on an anchor by using the words "I can't" and "I wish I could"?

For more than forty years, I never learned to swim. Every time I was confronted with an invitation to go swimming, I would say, "I can't swim." The true response should have been: "I've never learned how to swim." As a non-swimmer, I would compare myself to someone who could swim and judge that person to be superior to me. The fact is, an "I can't" in one area triggers more of the same: "I can't get a job," "I can't find anyone to love me," and so on.

*By saying "I can't," you invite
yourself to feel inept, insufficient,
and negative about your abilities.*

Eventually, I learned to swim at the YMCA. I earned the right
to say, "I can swim." With practice, I became better at it,
although I am by no means the greatest swimmer in the
ocean. However, as I improved as a swimmer, my self-image
and self-esteem improved.

When we give credence to our critics and permit them to shape the image we have of ourselves, we discount our abilities to learn, achieve, and excel. Create your own belief system and feel the power of the words "I can" and "I will."

A sure cure for low self-esteem is to achieve something on your own. With your accomplishment, you prove something to yourself and the universe. You show the world that you can do what you set out to do. It's like playing pinball or computer games: every time you get past an obstacle and solve a problem for yourself, you chalk up personal points toward higher self-esteem. So score one for you. Decide you are a "can-do" person, and you will become a "will-do" person.

Each crisis you get through makes you stronger. The more heavy lifting you do, the stronger you get and the more capable you are of coping with the next crisis. Success comes from getting up each time you fall and not giving up each time you fail, until you don't fall or fail anymore. In fact, you start to succeed when you start out to succeed. Bounce back, don't roll over!

Tearing Down vs. Building Up

Have you ever noticed how some people seem to enjoy pulling others down? What a world this would be if every human being recognized the value of every other human being and helped to pull others up instead of down! You can start the ball rolling toward a better world by recognizing your own value.

Consider for a moment all the great thinkers and scientists; the great poets, playwrights, painters, and statesmen; the accomplished builders, business tycoons, athletes, and astronauts. They were or are all just human. They were born as humans; they ended or will end their lives as humans. They were or are pretty much the same inside as you.

Instead of putting yourself down, take stock of who you really are and what your capabilities are.

Begin with a thorough self-examination. Enumerate your best assets, your God-given assets. You'll find that you have a lot to work with. The only limits to your ability to discover and fulfill your dreams are those you place on yourself.

I came across this daily meditation in Iyanla Vanzant's book, *Acts of Faith*, which begins: "We have such poor images of ourselves that we have difficulty understanding the good others see in us." It went on to say that self-esteem begins when you accept compliments others give you, and self-confidence grows when you celebrate your small victories and successes. "It all begins with our willingness to acknowledge that we are really fine, just the way we are."

Accept the fact that it's okay to be you. It's great to be you!

When it comes to being you, nobody does it better. You're the best you there is. You are the only you there will ever be. Remember, you choose how you see yourself. When you decide to accept your own self-worth, you embark on a life of peace, fulfillment, and achievement. And once you're happy with yourself, you can expect others to find qualities they admire in you.

Is there something about yourself that you want to change? First accept who you are. Then decide what you want to change and what you are going to do to achieve it.

There's no sense in wallowing in the negative when you could be doing something positive to improve your life.

Another way to find yourself is to give to others. Since I fly a lot, I'm familiar with the safety briefings aboard all the various airlines and their different types of aircraft. Typically when they explain how to don an oxygen mask, they tell you that if you're traveling with a small child, you should place the mask on yourself first before assisting the child. In my mind, there's a parallel to achieving self-esteem: you have to help yourself before you can help others. I truly believe that life is about serving others, but you have to serve yourself before you have the capacity or wherewithal to be of service to anyone else.

Escaping Our Past

Some of us are conditioned by our past, but it makes no sense to keep reliving the past. I have learned to look at the past as a notebook or template that needs to be opened up and written upon. It's up to each of us to take our past and improve on it.

Are you living in the past today? Are you letting past negative experiences influence the choices you make in your daily life today?

Many people have trouble separating what they do and what happens to them from who they are. They think they are their behavior. You are not your behavior. You are separate from and more than your behavior. However, when you begin to appreciate the fantastic being that you are, you will also begin to see a change in your behavior. Coming to terms with our past helps us to love ourselves, which changes how we relate to others in our world.

When something unexpected happens, we have to look at it from a distance. By separating ourselves from our experiences, we are able to move on with our lives. If we don't, we're stuck in the puddle of the past without a paddle.

You are not your parents' divorce. You are not a lost job, a lost love, or a lost opportunity.

In one of his talks on dharma, the Buddhist teacher Thich Nhat Hanh explained that mindfulness, or being conscious of your thoughts and actions, can overcome negative thoughts about yourself that have become habitual. Positive thinking can also overcome fear, anguish, anxiety, and despair. "Our joy, our peace, our happiness depend very much on our practice of recognizing and transforming our habit energies," he said. When negative thoughts come to mind, you should recognize them and, in this way, take control of the situation. Don't fight the negativity to the point where you hate yourself more, just alert yourself to it and work on the negativity until you can wrap it with a positive energy that springs up naturally.

If you take time to examine your past, you'll see it for what it is: the past. Sure, we can learn from the past, and philosophers say those who don't learn from history are condemned to make the same mistakes again and again. Come to think of it, when it comes to managing my business affairs, I have made the same mistakes or, if you will, experienced the same "growth opportunities" more than once or twice. However, I have learned that we travel in the present.

Our past can only go with us at our invitation, and we do ourselves a favor if we don't invite it along.

Go it alone in the present tense. Neither the past nor the future are places you can visit. The only place you can go is the present: today.

Learning from Mistakes

The Irish writer Oscar Wilde once quipped, "Experience is simply the name we give our mistakes." We all make mistakes, but a bigger mistake is harping on them until they drive you wild. A singer will record the same song many times. Each recording is called a take. Let's say that after the 99th recording, the producer asks everyone to listen to take 99. Everyone listens with one goal in mind: how to improve take 99. No one condemns it or judges it. After everyone gives his or her input, the producer says, "All right everyone, places, we're rolling, take 100." Take 99 was not a failure; it was just a *mis-take*. Life is just a series of takes that we sometimes call experience. Inherent in each take (experience) is a lesson. Learn the lesson and move on.

Mistakes happen and misfortune strikes even the most cautious planners and the luckiest of gamblers. I'm not going to tell you that the major missteps or growth opportunities of my life made me happy. I have tasted the bitterness of disappointment time and again. However, I believe that each and every experience, good or bad, creates new and exciting opportunities.

If you can find at least one positive outcome in each instance of adversity and focus on the positive, before long, from the bitterness will come sweetness.

You've heard it said that the bigger they are, the harder they fall. But sometimes the harder you fall, the stronger you become. It's called process. You can't change your past, but you can accept it and maybe even profit from it. The faster you process your unfortunate experiences and identify your positive outcomes, the faster your life will become a happy one. In my years of encounters with bad experiences, I've learned that nothing is ever as bad as it might first seem. I don't care how bad you think it is, it's always better than that.

After I was a big success with the original Famous Amos Chocolate Chip Cookie Company, I was a big failure, at least in Fortune 500 terms. I lost Famous Amos. I then launched several companies and products that for one reason or another did not have a very long shelf life or any profit in the profit and loss statement. At one point toward the end of the last millennium, the IRS was hounding me for money I didn't have to pay back taxes on companies I didn't have, and the banks were after me for missed mortgage payments on the one home I did have. It wasn't a pretty financial picture.

And get this: in 1992, I was legally barred from using my own name to sell cookies or cookie-related products. I not only lost my cookie company and my nickname, "Famous Amos," but I also lost the right to use my real name. I became a man without a name. Through it all — the business missteps, the IRS, the debts, and the loss of my name for two or three years — I was happy. I was even joyful. I was happy about myself and who I was, happy about my relationships — with my wife, Christine, my children, my friends, my community, and my beliefs. I was satisfied to have oodles of non-monetary wealth. These were riches beyond my wildest dreams, and these assets were non-taxable!

Who would have imagined that twenty-seven years after my mother and father divorced in Florida, I would make my mark selling chocolate-chip cookies in California? How could I have envisioned that decades after dropping out of high school, I would become a spokesman for the General Education Diploma (GED)?

Everything happens for good.

I really believe that. If I didn't, I'd just be wasting my time wondering why things didn't happen.

If Looks Could Kill

Physical appearance, or what we perceive our appearance to be, has a direct effect on our self-image and self-esteem. Adults invariably cluck and coo at newborns and say, "How cute," no matter how much the babies look like Winston Churchill or Eddie Murphy playing the puffed-up Nutty Professor. Can you remember the first time someone looked at you and ruled on how you looked — beautiful, gorgeous, shapely, fat, skinny, ugly, funny-looking? Did you ever wonder who empowered the "lookism" magistrates of our society to pass judgment on others?

It's a sad commentary on our society that conditioning starts so early, with beauty pageants for toddlers and preteens, and the awarding of crowns for symmetrical facial features and perfect body figures never ends.

If judging others by their covers rather than their contents was limited to a few panels of beauty contestant judges, it wouldn't be so bad. Unfortunately, prejudice based on looks is prevalent in all our information and entertainment media. There's little anyone can do to rein in the dream merchants of Hollywood and the image mongers of Madison Avenue.

It is almost laughable to think that a small fraternity of media moguls has conditioned hundreds of millions of people to want to look the ways these nameless, faceless people want them to look.

A Canadian study found that young girls view an average of 400 to 600 ads a day, which totals to as many as 25,000 by the time they're seventeen. It also found that the female models in those ads typically weigh 23 percent less than the average woman. It's no wonder so many teenage girls buy into the "beauty myth" that being skinny or shapely is a prerequisite to being attractive and loved. Worse yet, girls with low-esteem, which may result from their fear of measuring up to the images they see in the media, may develop deadly eating disorders.

There was a time when I did not like my physical appearance. I confess that I wanted to look like a television or movie star even though at the time, all television and movie stars were white, and there was no way I could change the color of my skin. Ultimately, I knew I couldn't change the way I looked, but I did change the way I felt. It took me years to get over my outward appearance. I started by looking at myself in the mirror, reminding myself that I had some nice features, and I built on that. Then I realized that I am the best-looking Wally Amos that ever lived.

Why not confound the conglomerates that spend millions of dollars a day trying to make you buy something to make you look or feel better, and save yourself a lot of money and angst, by making yourself feel better?

Avoid the trap of expecting to be treated a certain way because of who or what you appear to be.

The Nobel Peace Prize–winning activist Nelson Mandela, who helped defeat the apartheid system that had kept his fellow Africans in submission for a century, said: "It is what we make out of what we have, not what we are given, that separates one person from another." Expect the treatment you deserve for being the fully-evolved human being you really are.

Perhaps you've evolved to the point where you accept most everything about your body and only dislike one part that's either too small or too big or too straight or too crooked. You could spend thousands of dollars on plastic surgery and risk your good health for the rest of your life, or you could *get over it and accept it*!

Acceptance is a powerful tool in building self-esteem.

Once you have acceptance, you can gently begin to change what you don't like about yourself. Being able to laugh at yourself is another step toward positive self-esteem. If you can see humor in something you've done, you can forgive yourself, shake it off, and move on. Laughter is good both for the soul and for self-esteem.

Changing for Good

One of the first questions someone asks when they first meet you is "What do you do?" It's understood to mean "What do you do for a living?" or "How do you earn money?" When you think about it, if this country weren't so shackled by eighteenth-century Puritan values and repressive work ethics, we would ask "What do you do?" and we would mean "What do you do for fun?" or "What do you do to enjoy life?" or "What do you do to make people laugh, to make the world a better place, to spread love around the planet?"

Children barely able to stand on their two little feet are asked "What do you want to be?" As soon as they can speak, they are programmed to say they want to be a doctor, lawyer, firefighter, or maybe even stockbroker. In response to the question "What do you want to be?" they could instead be tutored to say, "I want to be happy," or "I want to be positive," or "I want to be well-adjusted, creative, filled with imagination, generous, grateful, helpful, and full of faith," or "I want to be in awe of the universe."

As an insecure adolescent and an immature young job seeker, I stumbled and slid from one position to another without getting a clue as to who I was. In 1989, after my ownership position in the Famous Amos cookie business crumbled, I was given a job as company spokesperson for $225,000 a year. It was a cushy job, but I didn't like representing people I didn't like. I could have skulked around for three years on that contract and salary, but I walked away with my head held high. Some people stay at one job for twenty or thirty years or more. It's easy to admire them for their dedication and "stick-to-itiveness" — if their work fulfills them, rewards them, challenges them, makes them feel good, or makes their community or their world a better place. Clinging to a meaningless job for the sheer security of having one is a different story.

You can spend a lifetime in a slot where there is no room to wiggle, waiting for a gold watch. Or you can roll out of that slot and on to something else, someplace else, half a block or half a world away.

We grow up believing it's bad to be a quitter, that winners never quit and quitters never win. I think there's a win in getting out while the getting is good and terminating an interminable situation before you pay the toll of an entire lifetime. Good timing may be the key to everything, but good timing can only be seen in hindsight. When I decided to start Famous Amos, the price of sugar was at an all-time high and the U.S. economy wasn't so hot. Common sense and backseat drivers all over L.A. told me it wasn't the right time to start a business. I sped on anyway, leaving the naysayers in the back seat, and the rest is cookie business history.

You probably don't realize it, but what you're doing now is preparing you for what you're going to do next. What you're doing now may not seem important to your future, but it could lead to doing something better.

There's a lot to be said for taking pride in what you do. If you're not proud or pleased with what you're doing or how you're doing it, look up at the clock to see if there's a sign that says "Time to Move On."

Your job, what you do for money, is not the same as you. Your source of financial security is not necessarily the source of your inner security. If you can't find satisfaction and enjoyment in what you're doing, what's the sense of doing it? If you don't enjoy how you make your money, find another way. The reward is in the doing and being. You can always find another way, legally, to make money.

Recently, I asked my friend, who is an internationally renowned heart surgeon, why he became a doctor. He said he enrolled in a pre-med course at a university to keep his parents from sending him to another school that specialized in engineering. His ad hoc anti-engineering school decision changed his life and positively changed the lives of many of his patients.

Because I give a lot of lectures, I am continually reviewing my life and looking for the lessons learned from living life every day. In retrospect, the times when I thought I was in total control were the times when I was more or less out of control. Like my heart-surgeon friend, the major, life-changing decisions of my life were never planned. They just happened. They were the wonderful, serendipitous experiences of life, seeds blown by the wind, which blossomed into something sweeter than what I had in mind.

On Being Worthy

In February 2005, the *Des Moines Register* reported that the state of Iowa was planning to spend six million dollars on a two-year advertising campaign to boost the state's self-esteem. Imagine an entire state with an inferiority complex! "Part of the problem is that we're humble," said the state official named to oversee the campaign. In my humble view, humility is a virtue that poses no threat to positive self-esteem. I hope and pray that Iowans will take notice of the state-sponsored ads, appreciate what they have, and help their home state elevate its self-image.

Even outside of Iowa, some people harbor the unspoken, unacknowledged feeling that they do not deserve to be happy or have their dreams come true. Maybe this is why we laughed along with Mike Myers in *Wayne's World* when he uttered his gag line, "We're not worthy!"

I believe we are worthy of anything we can will ourselves to become and work to achieve.

You cannot change yourself without first accepting who you are. Then you can decide what you want to change and what you are going to do about it.

Of course, you can't fulfill your life's dream unless you have one to fulfill. This is not an original thought. In the ever-popular 1950s Broadway musical *South Pacific*, the quirky character Bloody Mary tries to persuade a young U.S. Navy lieutenant to forget about war and spend his days enjoying her Bali Hai paradise. In the song "Happy Talk," she sings: "You gotta have a dream. If you don't have a dream, how you gonna have a dream come true?"

Obviously, if I hadn't had a dream of selling cookies on the Sunset Strip, it never would have happened.

Think about it: if you can see it, you can be it.

Of course, you won't be it overnight because being it takes more than just seeing it. That's where some of those other key ingredients come in: commitment, enthusiasm, and faith.

His Holiness the Dalai Lama, the spiritual and temporal leader of Tibetan Buddhists, began a talk on self-reliance with these words: "Within all beings there is a seed of perfection. However compassion is needed in order to activate that seed, which is inherent in our hearts and minds." In *The Art of Happiness*, the Dalai Lama suggests that the way to avoid loneliness and isolation is to look for positive attributes in everyone you meet and approach them in a positive way, with compassion in your mind. In this manner, all the positives will add up: yours, theirs, and the positive nature of the universe. I believe that self-esteem and love are intertwined. You've got to love yourself before you can love anyone. If you think of yourself as an individual expression of God or a priceless work of God's art, you'll find it easy to love yourself and pass that love on to others.

Why is it that so many people are obsessed with being "in control"? They work at making every part of their lives perfect. They have elaborate plans and strategies for accomplishing every little thing, short-term and long-term. I know of someone who bought a small townhouse apartment and has been working on it for a couple of years already, putting off moving in because she wants it to be perfect. In the meantime, she's paying rent somewhere else and doesn't get to enjoy living in her new, admittedly not-yet-perfect place.

Don't stress. Slow down.
Anything worth doing is worth
taking the time to do right.
Life can be a cakewalk if you
take time out to smell the cookies.

The lesson of the ages is to never give up hope, because the universe acts in mysterious ways. A man in my little town lost his high school ring back in 1974. He searched all over town for days and weeks. Years later, he still stopped at garage sales, hoping to find it. Twenty-six years after he lost his treasured ring, a woman in Sioux Falls, South Dakota, saw an item gleaming in the dirt in her backyard, which was located over 3,000 miles from Kailua High School. She called the school and described the initials that had been engraved in the 1974 class ring. The next day she contacted its owner and arranged to have it returned to him in Hawaii.

Fulfilling Dreams

Years ago the world seemed a simpler place. I remember Doris Day sang the song "Que Sera Sera" about a daughter who asked her mother, "Will I be pretty? Will I be rich?" and, of course, the mother replied, "Whatever will be, will be." When the daughter grew up and had children of her own, her son asked, "Will I be handsome? Will I be rich?" As children, we're conditioned to believe that good looks and money can bring happiness. As adults, we're conditioned to believe that if you win the lottery, you don't need the good looks because large amounts of money can solve all your problems and you'll live happily ever after. Still, many lottery winners end up broke and sad in a short period of time.

For several years, I was part of the Hollywood lifestyle of flashing your cash and showing off your status symbols and designer goods. But having material things did not give me a sense of satisfaction or accomplishment. I tell people that I was *in* show business but not a *part* of it.

What I learned is that if money is all that matters to you, you'll never have enough and you won't be happy with any less.

If you rely on material things to give meaning to your life, you'll be miserable when you see that someone else's stuff is even better and more expensive than your stuff. Life would be so simple if we could be satisfied as easily as the lyrics of this Dave Clark Five song suggest: "Give me one kiss and I'll be happy... Just, just to be with you."

It's wonderful to dream sweet dreams of kisses to come. There's also some sweetness to be had in living in the moment. If you don't make up your mind to live life to the fullest now, you probably never will; if you're not having fun now because you're waiting, just waiting, for your dream to come true, you likely never will.

It's a certainty that tomorrow and every day will have twenty-four hours. What you choose to do with them is up to you.

Why wait till you hit retirement age, or whatever age you have in mind, to enjoy life? Imagine how very sad it will be at that age to look back and say, "I wish I'd done more when I was younger. I wish I'd taken more trips. I wish I'd pursued that hobby or pastime or played the kazoo more often when I was younger." Well, you're younger than that age now, so what's your excuse?

Having fun is a choice. Taking charge of your life is a choice. So why not choose now? Choose to start having fun today! Choose to make the most of every day. Choose to discover and fulfill your life dreams.

Raising Your Self-Esteem

Here's a dozen — make it a (cookie) baker's dozen — tips on how to discover and fulfill your dreams:

1. Stop being your own worst enemy. Be your own best friend.

2. Don't put yourself down. Pull yourself up.

3. Don't permit others to define who you are. You cannot be a failure without your own consent.

4. Respect yourself. Place a high value on yourself.

5. Take stock of who you are and what you're capable of. Work on weaknesses and find new strengths every day.